RIFF

BY LAURENCE FISHBURNE

★

★

DRAMATISTS
PLAY SERVICE
INC.

SPECIAL NOTE

Anyone receiving permission to produce RIFF RAFF is required to give credit to the Author as sole and exclusive Author of the Play on the title page of all programs distributed in connection with performances of the Play and in all instances in which the title of the Play appears for purposes of advertising, publicizing or otherwise exploiting the Play and/or a production thereof. The name of the Author must appear on a separate line, in which no other name appears, immediately beneath the title and in size of type equal to 50% of the size of the largest, most prominent letter used for the title of the Play. No person, firm or entity may receive credit larger or more prominent than that accorded the Author. The following acknowledgment must appear on the title page in all programs distributed in connection with performances of the Play:

Produced by Circle Repertory Theater
New York City

The premiere performance of RIFF RAFF
was produced by The LOA Productions in Los Angeles, California

For my beloved Brooklyn,
Peace.

RIFF RAFF was first produced by LOA Productions, Inc. (Laurence Fishburne and Jay Roberts, Producers) at Theatre GEO, in Los Angeles, California, on November 17, 1994. It was directed by Laurence Fishburne; the set and lighting designs were by Russell Pyle; the costume design was by Darryle Johnson; the sound design was by Steve Williams; the fight choreography was by Eddie Watkins; and the stage manager was Stephanie S. Scott. The cast was as follows:

"20/20" MIKE SAUNDERS .... Laurence Fishburne
BILLY "TORCH" MURPHY .... Titus Welliver
TONY "THE TIGER" RAWLINS .... Heavy D

RIFF RAFF was produced by Circle Repertory Theatre (Austin Pendleton, Artistic Director; Milan Stitt, Executive Director; Andrew Chipok, Managing Director) in New York City, in September, 1995. It was directed by Laurence Fishburne; the set design was by Edward T. Gianfrancesco; the costume design was by Michael Krass; the lighting design was by Dennis Parichy; the sound design was by Darron L. West; the fight director was Rich Sordelet; and the production stage manager was Greta Minsky. The cast was as follows:

"20/20" MIKE LEON .... Laurence Fishburne
BILLY "TORCH" MURPHY .... Titus Welliver
TONY "THE TIGER" LEE .... Heavy D

AUTHOR'S NOTE

My intention when writing this play was to create a very intense exercise for myself as an actor. It became, in part at least, something of an exorcism. It is my belief that we all as human beings possess our own particular demons. Or are possessed by them at one time or another. The characters in this play represent those demons which I faced in my youth. Therefore, I should like to make the following suggestions to those of you about to *Riff.*

First: Always, always, always after lights up, begin the play with a flame. A light, a candle, a match; it makes no difference which. Demons have always been aroused by fire and recognize it as a sign that they are free to take the stage and play.

Secondly: A flame should always be lit at Tony's exit at the end of scene four. This will ensure a safe return home for our demons until the next performance.

Third: With respect to race, or perhaps more appropriately to cultural origins; it is my hope, my wish and my desire that *Riff Raff* should be performed by as many varieties of human beings as is produced by the species. In short, I don't care what you look like. As long as you sound like you're from Brooklyn, fine.

Lastly: As mentioned before, this is largely an exercise for actors. So, for those of you who may or may not think of yourselves as courageous and confident cats; practitioners of the craft, be forewarned: DON'T FUCK AROUND! COME CORRECT, COME TO GET DOWN. A "RIFF" IS A "RIFF." SO SWING!

CHARACTERS

"20/20" MIKE LEON, 30s
BILLY "TORCH" MURPHY, 30s
TONY "THE TIGER" LEE, 30s

TIME

The Present, All Hallows Eve, 9:00 P.M.

PLACE

Corner third floor apartment, abandoned building on New York's Lower East Side

SETTING

There is an ugly, legless couch sitting under two windows to one side of the room. An old chair sits on two legs under two windows to the other side. There is a make-shift table in front of the chair and couch. White candles, burnt to the nub and half-burnt are stuck to several hubcaps strewn about the apartment, the table, floor, window sills, etc. There is a small bathroom off to one side of the room with busted-up fixtures. The place is strewn with debris: burnt matches, cotton balls, and empty crack vials. There are crumpled up small to medium brown paper bags, coffee cups, cigarette butts, bottles, cans, take-out food containers, sterno cans, coffee cans, etc. There is a door-less closet that houses a urine stained mattress which stands on end. A street light can be seen from the windows behind the couch; its light spills into the room, illuminating it. The faint sounds of the street can be heard: traffic, sirens, shouts and the like....

RIFF RAFF

Scene 1

Nine o'clock at night.

As the lights come up we hear the sound of two sets of feet running up the stairs. First one, then two. The leaders pace is quick, hurried, in a frenzy. The second is slow, deliberate, and fatigued.

"20/20" Mike Leon enters. He is in his early thirties. He wears a white lab coat, stained with blood, khaki pants and sneakers. He carries a black briefcase.

MIKE. Okay ... we made it.... Okay ... okay, okay, okay, okay. Okay, you made it. You made it, Mikey. Now all you gotta do is calm down. Just calm the fuck down and try to think, baby ... gotta think.... You just gotta think. Hey, Billy, what do you think, huh? Where the fuck are you?... Hey Billy, come on. Come on, Billy! Yo Torch. Hurry up, hurry up! Come on, you can make it. You're almost there. You can make it, bro!!

TORCH. *(Offstage.)* Don't fucking call me that! I'm coming. I'm coming!!! Keep your shirt on Mikey. It's fucking dark in here. Can't hardly see nothing. You sure we're gonna be safe up here?

MIKE. Yeah I'm sure! *(Billy "Torch" Murphy enters. He is in his early thirties. He wears a black leather jacket, white T-shirt, black jeans and motorcycle boots. He has a Halloween mask on his head and keeps one hand in his jacket pocket.)*

TORCH. Holy shit! This is it?

MIKE. Yeah!

TORCH. This is your fucking hide-out?

MIKE. Yeah, yeah; this is it. Go ahead, sit down. Make yourself at home.
TORCH. And you're sure Manny won't come looking for us here?
MIKE. Yeah, yeah, I'm sure.
TORCH. You positive?
MIKE. Absolutely. Absolutely positive.
TORCH. Yeah well, let me tell you something, looks like quite a few people found your little hide-away, pal.
MIKE. Will you just go ahead and sit down.
TORCH. Yeah, yeah, I'll do that. But let me tell you something else, I sure as shit ain't gonna take my shoes off in this joint. God forbid I catch fucking AIDS.
MIKE. The fucks the matter with you? We're alright. Ain't we? We're safe for the time being. Nobody saw us get off the train. Nobody saw us come in here. What are you so fucking worried about? Huh?
TORCH. I don't know Mike. I don't know about this place. I don't know if I feel safe, us staying here. What if Manny and his boys find us? What about that, huh? What are we gonna do then?
MIKE. I told you, I told you; we're safe. This place is like fucking Fort Knox. Nobody comes in or out unless they know the way. Me and my man Tony used to hide out here all the time.
TORCH. Yeah, yeah you keep saying that. You sure nobody saw us?
MIKE. Yeah I'm sure ... Jesus this place is a mess.
TORCH. No shit. Hey look, I don't know if I like this Mike. I think we should blow; I think we should get the fuck out of here.
MIKE. And do what? Ride the fucking subway till somebody spots us; or better yet kills us?
TORCH. We take our chances on the street, we're better off I'm telling you.
MIKE. Forget about it. We got no bread, no wheels and half the dealers on the east side looking for us. Not to mention the cops.

TORCH. Yeah man, but we got to do some fucking thing. I mean, we got to at least get out of New York. Head to Jersey, Philly.... Maybe Miami; I hear the weather is nice down there.

MIKE. Miami? What are you fucking crazy? Forget about it. Manny's got too many connections on the East Coast. We got to go out west. California, Seattle, maybe.

TORCH. Look, we got three keys of the best smack that money can buy. We gotta be able to do something with it right? Step on it a few times you know? Sell it to somebody. Maybe this guy Tony; your friend you called.

MIKE. No way man, no way. He's just gonna help us get out of town, that's all. Tony's out of the life now.

TORCH. Let me tell you something, once you had a taste of the life, that's it. Once in the life, always in the life, Mikey.

MIKE. No way ... not my man Tony, he's out; married, got a kid the whole nine ... lucky motherfucker. We used to come up here all the time. Fucking Freddy was always asking us to bring him up here.

TORCH. Fucking Freddy ... some piece of work he is. Catch that motherfucker, throw him off a roof.

MIKE. I can't believe he left us hanging in Far Rockaway.

TORCH. Fuck "Freddy Nine-Lives"!!! Cock sucker said the job was easy ... said it was gonna be a cinch. Now look at us. Sitting here in some fucking firetrap.

MIKE. It would've been a cinch if you had chilled the fuck out!

TORCH. Here we go! Don't fucking start with me Mikey!!

MIKE. I can't believe you fucking shot a kid.

TORCH. It was do or die, Mikey! How many fucking times you gonna say it?

MIKE. You fucking shot a kid! I can't believe that.

TORCH. Forget about it will you? What's done is done. *(Pause.)*

MIKE. Yeah ... yeah right, how's your hand bro?

TORCH. It's bleeding. And stop calling me that. I ain't your brother!

MIKE. Oh! So it's like that now?

TORCH. You bet your ass it is.

MIKE. You're a sick man, Mr. Williams.
TORCH. Hey! I told you not to call me that.
MIKE. Yep, you're a very sick man.
TORCH. I'm not sick. I just got a cold ... my fucking hand is killing me. *(Pause.)*
MIKE. Come on Tony, where are you?
TORCH. Come on, let's get out of here. Fuck this sitting on our asses waiting for your friend to show up. God forbid Manny's boys should find us; forget about it. They'll fucking have us for breakfast.
MIKE. Yo.... Yo.... Be quiet. What was that?
TORCH. What?
MIKE. Listen. The fuck is that? *(We hear a loud screeching sound offstage.)*
TORCH. The fuck should I know? Maybe it's your friend.
MIKE. Nah, something else. I know I heard that sound before.
TORCH. So what are you asking me about it for? I don't...
MIKE. Ssshhh ... *(Pause.)* Oh shit!
TORCH. What?
MIKE. I fucking hate that.
TORCH. Hate what? What is it?
MIKE. Fucking rat.
TORCH. A fucking rat; you sure?
MIKE. Yeah. I'm sure
TORCH. You positive?
MIKE. Absolutely. Absolutely positive.
TORCH. How do you know for sure? How do you know it's not ...
MIKE. Wait a second ... listen ... listen.
TORCH. Don't do that.
MIKE. That's a fucking rat. I heard it once, I heard it a million times before. Man I hate rats! I can't stand them shits. I remember one time I was dating this girl lived down by Mill Basin. Candy Brown ... bitch was fine, bro.
TORCH. I told you not to call me that.
MIKE. I mean fine!! This chick was so fine I spent all the bread I could get my hands on trying to get into her panties.

Took her to Coney Island, to the aquarium, the movies. Anyplace in Brooklyn where I thought she might give it up, that's where I'd take her, right? So after we went out a few times, I don't know to this day how I knew, but I could tell that she had decided to give me some right? So we had gone to the movies over on Church Ave and when the flick was over she asked me to walk her home right? So I go like: "bet." So we start walking toward Mill Basin. Like we walking and talking you know, shooting the breeze and ping, ping, my 20/20 starts going off like crazy!! I could feel all the fellas around her way checking me out like.... "Who's this chump and what's she doing with him?" I'm looking over my shoulder, watching my back and shit 'cause I lived in the projects over in East New York and ain't never been to Mill Basin before, so I'm scared right. But I'm playing it off like I ain't, 'cause I don't want her to think I'm a punk. Anyway, when we finally get to her building and it's all run down and shit, I'm like; what the fuck is a chick this fine doing living in a place like this. I mean the whole building smelled like piss, the stairs sounded like they would cave in under your feet. Hallways was all dark and shit. Some of the other apartments was all burnt out.

TORCH. Whoa!! Déjà vu.

MIKE. Yeah. So I'm thinking; "What the fuck am I doing here? I'm miles from home and probably can't even find my way back."

TORCH. I know the feeling.

MIKE. But I'm like, "This girl is fine as wine." Dress her up in garbage bags, put TV dinners on her head, you could not hide this kind of beauty. And after I had taken her out all them times! Shit, I was gonna get them panties ... I mean, I was serious about this pussy, okay?

TORCH. Is there a point to this story?

MIKE. Yo, check it. We had stopped and got some Bacardi on the way right? And when we get to her apartment on the fourth floor? The shit was hooked up! Top to bottom, all exotic and shit, beads hanging over the bedroom door, different colored light bulbs in the ceiling, pillows on the floor, that type of shit; right? She lit up a joint, some incense and asks me to make us some drinks while she goes and gets comfortable. I'm like, *Papi chulo number 1! Aqui estoy, hoy es mi dia!!* I made it to Mill Basin alive and I'm gonna fuck the finest girl I ever seen in my whole life. So I make the drinks, right, one for me, one for her. And I'm sitting on the floor sipping mine, taking it all in, you know? The reefer, the lights, the incense and ping, ping, my 20/20 goes off again. It was like I could feel something in the room. Check it out, I go to put my drink down, right? The shit spills over! Yo, the fucking floor was slanted, bro, no lie. Shit was like this. So now I'm trying to clean up my mess and I hear this scratching sound on the floor behind me; right? I turned around and I see this rat. Fucking rat this big, I swear to God. It was big as your fucking head. Arrr, I can't stand them shits. Yo, that shit blew my mind. I'm telling you, I couldn't concentrate on nothing else for the whole rest of the night. See what happened was, when I was little, my sister Debbie got bit by a rat. She was only 2 or 3 years old at the time and she almost died from it. I didn't know it then, but I had kept that shit locked up in the back of my mind. Like in my sub-conscience, you know? So when the chick came out of the bathroom, all ready to go and looking fine as a motherfucker; man, pussy was the furthest thing from my mind. *(Pause. Mike seems to sense something outside; he rises and moves to a window.)* About time! Yo here he comes.

TORCH. Who?

MIKE. My man. "Tony the Tiger."

TORCH. You sure?

MIKE. I got eyes in the back of my head, bro. 20/20 Mike; that's me. Besides, I'd know that walk anywhere. Yo look outside.

TORCH. What for?

MIKE. See if anybody's on that side. Somebody might have followed him.

TORCH. Fuck you. You want to look go ahead. My fucking hand's killing me.

MIKE. Hey, will you just stick your head out the window, take a look around, okay?

TORCH. Yeah, yeah, sure ... take it easy ... I don't see the use in all this "I Spy" shit. Fuckin "Maniac" probably already knows where we're hiding anyway. *(Pause. Torch rises and looks out the window.)*

MIKE. He don't know jack-shit. Come on T.

TORCH. Yeah, says you.

MIKE. Yeah, says me. *(Pause.)* You see anybody?

TORCH. There's two guys on the corner by the pay phone.

MIKE. Fuck!!

TORCH. What's taking your friend so long.

MIKE. He's almost here; he's crossing the street.

TORCH. We ought to get out of here Mike.

MIKE. Shut-up. I'm trying to think of something.

TORCH. While you're doing that I'm bleeding like a stuck pig ... I gotta take a leak ... *(Mike crosses to Torch and applies pressure to his hand.)*

MIKE.	TORCH.
Sit down and,	Oww-Oww!!!!
be quiet you stupid	Yeah! Alright!
fuck!	Get off of me!!

TORCH. Ah shit! Hey don't call me that. I don't like that shit.

MIKE. Shut-up! Okay. I'm trying to think!

TORCH. Well think faster asshole ... Jesus ... I gotta take a pisser!!

TONY. *(Offstage.)* Hey yo Mike!! *(Pause.)* Yo Mike!... Yo Mikey! Hey, yo Mike! You there?

TORCH. Oh, fuck. *(Pause.)*

MIKE. Okay. I'm gonna go up on the roof, check out the two guys by the pay phone.

TORCH. I'm coming with you. No way you leave me by myself. *(Torch starts to rise, Mike stops him.)*

MIKE. No, you move around too much you'll only make yourself bleed more, you stupid.

TORCH. Hey, I'm, gonna be stupid one more fucking time ...

MIKE. I'm sorry, okay ... I'm sorry.

TORCH. People been calling me stupid all my life!

MIKE. Okay, okay ... I said I was sorry ... Jesus! Just sit tight okay? I'm gonna just be up on the roof.
TORCH. I hate that shit.
TONY. *(Offstage, climbing the steps.)* Hey, yo Mike! What's up baby, where you at?
TORCH. I don't like this Mike. I don't know this guy.
MIKE. How many times I gotta tell you; he's a friend of mine.
TORCH. Yeah ... yeah you keep saying that. Big deal. He ain't no friend of mine. *(Mike takes a small hand gun from the briefcase and hands it to Torch.)*
MIKE. Look ... here take the piece back, okay? Keep it out if you want. I promise he won't fuck with you. I'll be right back. Don't let him leave, and whatever you do don't fucking shoot him okay?
TORCH. Where you going? Why you gotta leave?
MIKE. Billy ... Billy ... just keep it out, don't do anything stupid ...
TORCH. I ain't stupid!
TONY. *(Offstage.)* Come on Mike, I know you're up there. Mike? Mikey answer me! *(Pause.)*
MIKE. Answer him.
TORCH. What? *(Mike moves to the door.)*
MIKE. Go ahead. Answer him. I'm gonna check the roof.
TORCH. I don't know him ... Mikey ... I don't know this guy. *(Mike exits.)* Shit Mike; I'm sick man. Fuck, I gotta piss. *(Torch opens the briefcase and opens one of the kilos of heroin. He smells it, then he hastily snorts the heroin and then puts the kilo back ... he aims the pistol at the door as Tony enters. Tony Lee is in his early thirties. He is wearing a lightweight leather jacket, sport shirt and slacks.)*
TONY. Goddamn, this place is fucked up.
TORCH. Trick or treat, motherfucker! *(Tony raises his hands.)*
TONY. Hey, yo.... No problem baby. I'm cool. No problem.
TORCH. Shut-up and step into the middle of the floor there, slick; nice and easy. *(Tony moves to the C. of the room.)*
TONY. Right here okay chief?
TORCH. That's just fine, just fine. Hey fucker, use your

head. Empty your pockets on the table there ... be very, very careful. *(Tony empties his pockets.)*

TONY. Careful is my middle name man. Just don't shoot a brother, is all I'm saying.

TORCH. Just so long as the brother keeps his hands where I can see them. Now the jacket. *(Tony takes a cellular phone from his inside pocket.)*

TONY. No problem. That's all I got on me chief. I hate carrying this thing, but it keeps the old lady off my case, you know what I'm saying?

TORCH. Hey, I ain't interested in your life story pal. Sit down over there. Easy ... and keep your hands up. *(Pause. As Tony puts his phone away, sits in the chair.)*

TONY. Say, my man?

TORCH. The fuck do you want?

TONY. Mike here?

TORCH. The fuck should I know? *(Pause.)*

TONY. Didn't I hear two people up here?

TORCH. Gives a fuck what you heard? *(Pause.)*

TONY. I'm just trying to make sure I'm in the right place, that's all. He called my old lady and said he was trying to find his sister Debbie. I just want to see if I can help the brother out.

TORCH. Great, another one with the brother shit. Ouch.... Fucking hand. *(Pause.)*

TONY. Hey man, you alright?

TORCH. Take it easy you.

TONY. Hey no problem ... look man, I mean, I know I don't know you, but you look kinda like ... sick.

TORCH. I'm fine, I just got a cold is all. I'm fine. You just take it easy.

TONY. No problem. Damn, this place is fucked up. Junkies done come in here and left shit everywhere.

TORCH. Fucking hate junkies.

TONY. I mean the place was always kind of funky, but I don't remember it being this bad. *(Pause.)*

TORCH. You been here before?

TONY. Oh yeah. Me and Mike used to hide out here all

the time.
TORCH. Keep your fucking hands up!!
TONY. Had it hooked up pretty nice too. *(Pause.)*
TORCH. So you're a friend of his, huh?
TONY. Yo, that's my motherfucking man! We go back like car seats baby. Too much crime, too much time; you know what I'm saying?
TORCH. Oh Jesus, well I hope you have a nice reunion.... Christ almighty.
TONY. You alright man?
TORCH. Yeah I'm fine! *(Pause.)* I gotta take a piss.
TONY. Go ahead man; take a break I ain't gonna give you no problem.
TORCH. You just be quiet till Mike gets back.
TONY. He's here?
TORCH. Yeah, yeah, he's up the roof. Said you was to wait for him till he comes down. Said to keep you here. Jesus, I gotta piss. *(Pause.)*
TONY. My man?
TORCH. What?
TONY. Can I put my hands down now?
TORCH. Yeah; but don't think I won't cap you one just 'cause you're a friend of Mikes.
TONY. No problem ... what's your name?
TORCH. What are we, fucking friends?
TONY. What's your name, man?
TORCH. Torch.
TONY. Tony-T. Nice to meet you.
TORCH. Whatever.
TONY. I seen you somewhere before?
TORCH. Never.
TONY. You sure? We never met before?
TORCH. Let me tell you something, fucker; I never seen you before and you never seen me. You understand? I don't know you, and I don't want to know you. I just as soon shoot you as look at you. Got it?
TONY. No problem.... It's cool, I'm not ... you the man, baby ... you the man.

TORCH. Put your fucking hands behind your head! Behind your head!!! Fucking Mikey ... Mikey, where are you, get down here, I got to take a leak. You hear me Mikey? You don't get down here fast, I'm gonna put one in your friend here. Aw fuck ...

TONY. Hey man, take it easy!!.

TORCH. You shut-up, just shut the fuck up. Aww.... Aww ... no ... no ... aw ... aw shit. *(Mike enters.)*

MIKE. Whoa ... Torch! Whoa ... easy ... Billy. Take it easy ... don't shoot, okay? Just gimme the gun ... that's it. You okay bro?

TORCH. Don't fucking call me that!! Aw fuck me!

MIKE. What's wrong Billy?... Tony what happened?

TONY. Think your boy had a little accident.

TORCH. I pissed my fucking pants man.

MIKE. Oh, shit, I'm sorry bro. Hey Billy sit down over here for a second, okay.

TONY. 20/20 Mike!

MIKE. Tony T. What's up, papi?

TORCH. Hey, fellas ... I could use a hand over here.

MIKE. Hey yo, chill ... how's Maxine?

TONY. Max is fine. She's kinda worried about you and your sister.

MIKE. How my God-daughter? How's Precious?

TONY. She's getting big, man; she'll be four next month.

MIKE. Four years old already! Damn!

TONY. Always asking for Uncle Mikey.

MIKE. Wow, that's beautiful.... Yo, what you been up to?

TONY. Nah. What you been up to? The fuck is wrong that my woman got to call me at the job.

MIKE. I'm sorry T, but I didn't know who else to call. Hey Max ain't mad, is she?

TONY. No, Max is cool. What's up Mike? Max said you couldn't find Debbie again.

MIKE. My sister?

TONY. Yeah Mike! Your sister, Debbie the dope fiend, you remember her, right? *(Pause.)*

MIKE. Oh shit! Yeah right, I'm sorry Tony. Yo listen Debbie's okay, she's okay, really, this ain't about her.

TONY. I knew it! I knew something was up when she told me you wanted to meet me in this fucking dump. Mike, what's up?

MIKE. My situations kinda fucked up and I just didn't want to start no shit that's all Tony. *(Pause.)* It's good to see you bro. Damn, it's almost three years.

TONY. Yeah. So I ain't down here trying to help you find Debbie?

TORCH. Hey fellas, can I get some help over here?

MIKE. Take it easy, Torch. Not exactly, Tony.

TONY. Then what's up?

TORCH. Fellas!!

MIKE. We'll get you cleaned up in a second!!! It's a long story. You see anybody following you?

TONY. Nah ... it's two dudes on the corner using the pay phone. Dealing, hanging out, you know. *(Pause.)* Yo Mike ... we cool?

MIKE. Yeah, we cool.

TONY. Bet. You OK, Torch?

TORCH. Fuck you. Fuck the both of youse ... cocksuckers ... I'm bleeding, my hand's killing me and I'm soaked to the gills in my own piss, for chrissake.

MIKE. Yo, Torch, take it easy.

TONY. I think I got some old sweats in my ride downstairs, alright? I'll bring them up and we can get you out of them pissy pants, get you cleaned up.

TORCH. Yeah, well, what are you waiting on? Hurry up. I'm dying over here.

TONY. Damn, Mike, where you find this evil motherfucker man.

MIKE. It's a long story T. Hey yo, can you get us something to eat? And maybe something to drink too?

TORCH. Yeah. Get some cigarettes and something sweet.

TONY. No problem.

MIKE. And maybe some stuff to clean up his hand, man. It's pretty fucked up.

TONY. No problem.... Yo Mike, what happened, man? The

fuck y'all do?

MIKE. We tried to beat somebody and ran into a little problem, that's all.

TONY. You try to beat somebody? Who?

MIKE. You don't want to know.

TORCH. Manny Rivera, that's who! We ripped him off for three keys of smack. Okay?

MIKE. Torch!! I thought we said we was gonna keep that to ourselves

TORCH. Come on Mike, half the city knows by now.

TONY. You did what?! Wait.... Wait, wait a minute man. You beat Manny Rivera for how many keys?

TORCH. Three. It was supposed to be four, but we lost one, what a fucking waste.

MIKE. You know you got a lot of nerve talking that shit after what you did to that kid?

TORCH. Don't you fucking start this shit with me again, Mikey!!

MIKE. What'd did you have to go shoot him for?

TORCH. Because the fucking guy was reaching for his piece!

MIKE. You so fucking stupid. I can't believe I let you talk me into this shit.

TONY. Yo chill!!! Manny Rivera? Three keys man.... What the fuck was y'all thinking about? Mike, you done fucked up, you know that.

MIKE. Yeah, tell me about it.

TORCH. Next time you call me stupid, I'm gonna ...

TONY. Manny Rivera finds you motherfuckers, it won't be no next time. *(Pause. Tony exits.)*

TORCH. Hey Mike, I'm not feeling too good man.

MIKE. Take it easy. Stop moving around so much, will you? Tony's gonna be back in a minute. Let me see that hand.

TORCH. I can't feel my fingers; aw shit, I feel like I'm gonna pass out.

MIKE. Jesus. You're all sweaty and shit.

TORCH. It's this fucking cold I'm trying to catch. I'll be fine.... Soon as we get out of here.

MIKE. Let me see that hand.

TORCH. No ... no just leave it alone, I'll be fine.
MIKE. Come on, let me see it, you keep it in your pocket it's gonna get infected.
TORCH. No it ain't. Come on Mikey stop it, let go my fucking arm for chrissake will ya?
MIKE. Okay.... Okay go ahead keep it in your pocket, bleed to death, stupid.
TORCH. Call me that again I'm gonna throw you a fucking beating you never forget! *(Mike moves to a window.)*
MIKE. Yeah right, with one fucking hand? Shit gets infected bad enough you'll get gangrene, they'll cut the fucking thing off.
TORCH. The fuck they will ... besides it ain't that bad.
MIKE. That's what you think fine. See if I give a marvelous when it falls off.
TORCH. It ain't gonna fall off. It ain't that bad. I'm telling you, it's just a scratch.
MIKE. Hold up a minute. Wha ... where the fuck?
TORCH. What? what's happening?
MIKE. They were there just a minute ago.
TORCH. Who?
MIKE. The two guys.
TORCH. By the pay phone?
MIKE. Yeah, but I don't see them no more.
TORCH. What about your friend, Frosted Flakes. You see him?
MIKE. No ... no, where the fuck? *(Mike exits to the hallway and then re-enters.)* They're gone.
TORCH. You sure?
MIKE. Yeah, I'm sure
TORCH. You positive?
MIKE. Absolutely. Absolutely positive.
TORCH. Look, I didn't want to say nothing about it, but I think I seen him before. I just can't remember where.
MIKE. Tony?
TORCH. Yeah.
MIKE. You sure?
TORCH. Yeah, I'm sure.

MIKE. You positive?
TORCH. Ahh ... I don't know, can't remember.
MIKE. How could you forget somebody like Tony?
TORCH. I don't know, but it'll come to me. I'll tell you one fucking thing for sure. I don't like him.
MIKE. You didn't like me when you met me, either, Mr. Williams.
TORCH. Cut me a break with the Mr. Williams shit.
MIKE. Sorry, bro.
TORCH. And stop calling me bro. Jesus, I only known you a month and already your like the biggest pain in the ass I've had my whole fucking life.
MIKE. That's only natural seeing as how you and me got the same *(Overlap next line.)* fucking father.
TORCH. You and me is different, period. What we got in common I don't want to talk about. What I want to know about is your friend, Fucking Frosted Flakes.
MIKE. "Tony the Tiger."
TORCH. What's the difference? We're talking about the same guy, right.
MIKE. Yeah right, what about him?
TORCH. How do you know you can trust him? See what I'm saying, how do you know he won't rat us out?
MIKE. No way ... no way he'd do that. Me and Tony did too much time for that.
TORCH. You sure?
MIKE. Yeah, I'm sure!
TORCH. You positive?
MIKE. Absolutely, absolutely positive.
TORCH. Yeah, okay ... *(Pause.)* Hey, you think they'd really cut my hand off?
MIKE. Let me see. Jesus ... looks like you lost a lot of blood.
TORCH. Yeah? You should've seen the other guy.
MIKE. Don't move. *(Mike tries to clean Torch's hand.)*
TORCH. Ouch ... ouch ... take it easy, it fucking hurts you know.
MIKE. Quit moving then.... We're lucky to be alive. Shit, you're bleeding like crazy. Stop fucking moving, Billy!

TORCH. You keep twisting my pinky. I told you it's killing me.
MIKE. I get your blood on me, I swear to my mother, I'm gonna ...
TORCH. What you afraid you might catch something? Don't worry, I been tested more times than I can count.
MIKE. Yeah, me too.
TORCH. That makes us one happy fucking family, huh?
MIKE. Yeah. I guess so. You're fucking sweating bullets, let's get this jacket off. Sit tight. *(Mike helps Torch out of his jacket.)*
TORCH. I'm all wet. Hey Mikey?
MIKE. What?
TORCH. You ain't gonna tell nobody I pissed my pants, are you?
MIKE. No!! I ain't gonna tell nobody you pissed your pants. Go head, lay down, Tony will be back in a minute.
TORCH. I like two pillows. *(Mike puts the pillows on the mattress and Torch lays down.)* So what's up with you and him? What's this too much crime, too much time shit about?
MIKE. It's like I said; too much crime and too much time. It's funny we even ended up being friends. We was supposed to have this big fight when we met.
TORCH. Yeah? The two of youse was supposed to fight? I would've paid good money to see you get your ass kicked.
MIKE. Ain't that much kung-foolishness in the world.
TORCH. I'd a paid.
MIKE. Yeah you and the guy who started it. Fuckin' Garrnett. He was a little guy with a big mouth, said he was Tony's cousin, but he wasn't, right? Lying-ass motherfucker, I couldn't stand him. Always running off at the mouth, fronting like he's the man and shit. See, what happened was, we was in the eighth grade, right? It was just before school was getting out for summer, I remember it was hot that day. And me and my boys was in the bathroom smoking cigarettes after lunch period, right? So fuckin Garrnett comes in with his boys, right? He's wearing a brand new leather jacket, talking shit about how he robbed it off somebody. About how he did this, that and the other thing to the guy, right.

So I'm standing there minding my business, blowing smoke out the window and I don't know, man ... I just couldn't take it no more. I mean like every day this guy comes into the bathroom talking shit like it's alright, you know? I mean I don't know if it was 'cause it was hot, or 'cause it was the last days of school. I'm telling you I hated them last days of school with a passion.
TORCH. With a vengeance, forget about it.
MIKE. Anyway, I says to Garrnett, I says to him, "What's the big deal, man? It's only a fucking jacket!" What the fuck I want to do that for? Everybody in the bathroom gets real quiet, right? Fucking Garrnett's got this crazy look on his face, like, I know you ain't talking to me, right? Next thing I know, the punk jumps up in my face, talking about he's going to kick my ass if I don't mind my business. Oh, man ... I picked him up and threw him head first right into the toilet. Motherfucker didn't know whether to shit or go blind, but that ain't stop him from running his mouth. "My cousin Tony's gonna kick your ass!" "Oh yeah? Fuck you and your whole fucking family!" "My cousin Tony's gonna make you sorry you ever messed with me, motherfucker!" "Go ahead, go get him! Tell him to meet me in Prospect Park tomorrow by the band shell. I'll throw him a beating he'll never fucking forget! Next day I'm up in the park waiting with a couple of my boys, see if his cousin would show up.... He don't, so I'm cool. I figure the little punk is lying as usual, right? Next thing I know everybody round my way is talking about some guy named Tony's looking for me, right? That he's into that kung fu, karate type shit and that he beat up on some of the Homicides from Coney Island, right? Yo, them cats was the craziest motherfuckers in Brooklyn! So now, I'm shitting bricks, right? Swear to God, bro, I'm bugging the fuck out, I got my switchblade and I'm looking all over the neighborhood for this guy. I checked Pino's Pizzeria, Carvelle's, Greasy Jack's, Hank's Joint ... nothing. So I'm standing across the street from Danny's Candy Store and ping, ping! My 20/20 starts going off like crazy, it's like I can feel somebody clocking me, right? I turn around and I see this guy standing there. And I could tell

from the look in his eyes that it's him. He says, "You Mike?" I says, "Yeah! You Tony?" He says, "Yeah." So now I got my hand in my pocket and I'm hoping like a motherfucker I get the switchblade out before this cat commences to kung fooing my ass, right? Next thing I know he says, "You want to go for a walk?" I swear to my mother I don't know to this day why I did, but I says, "Fuck it. Yeah, why not?" So we walking and talking about Garrnett, you know, and what an asshole he is. I mean like we were strangers to each other, but we wasn't, right? Yo ... we been like this ever since, went to Erasmus Hall, drank, smoked, got high! Ate at each others house all the time, you saw him, you saw me. My moms practically adopted him and my sister Debbie ... forget about it. She loved Tony. Senior year we got tired of going to school, dropped out and started doing crime. No stick-ups and none of that snatch and grab shit most of the cats our age was doing. Strictly flim-flam, bona fide money-making scams. I was the mouthpiece, Tony was the muscle. Man, we robbed motherfuckers blind! Made mad loot, crazy paper ... got busted, did a bullet on Riker's Island. I spent a whole eighteen months locked up with this dude. I don't know how I would have done my time without him. He used to recite this poem all the time; crazy jailhouse poetry, you know? That shit ... that shit really got me through, bro ... gave me the strength to hang in there and do my time. Then, when we got out and Maxine had Precious ... he asked me to be godfather. Me, bro, nobody but me! Damn, I can't believe she's almost four years old, like I ain't seen her in going on three years, that's a long time. Naw, man, fuck that noise, ain't no way Tony would rat us out.... Sheet.... That's my motherfucker! Too much crime ... too much time. You know what I'm saying?... Hey Torch, you okay? Torch, wake up man.... Tch. Come on man.... Oh, shit. *(Fade to black.)*

Scene 2

Around midnight.

Torch is in the chair, Tony is unpacking a bottle of rum, a six pack of Coke, and some Chinese take-out food on the table. Mike is in the bathroom.

MIKE. He was only a kid, man. A fucking kid. He wasn't going to shoot first. I'm telling you; He was bluffing.... He was scared.
TORCH. Like hell he was! He would've shot me and you both as sure as shit if I didn't get the drop on him.
MIKE. That's all you had to do; was get the drop on him. You didn't have to waste him. All you had to do was come in the room with the briefcase. Bring the briefcase in the room and set it down in front of the guy. But no you couldn't do that, could you? You had to shoot him, didn't you? You had to shoot a fucking kid.
TORCH. The guy was reaching for his piece. You saw him. What was I supposed to do? Let him blow my fucking brains out? He could have wasted us both. Then what? Huh? Maybe I should've let him blow us both away. How about that?
MIKE. You so fucking stupid, man. I never should have hooked up with you. I can't believe you shot a kid.
TORCH. Alright, that's it ... that's it! That's the last time you call me stupid. I'm gonna ...
MIKE. *(Moves to meet him.)* You gonna do what? Huh? Get the fuck out my face punk. What you gonna do without a gun in your hand? I ain't no kid, I'm a man! *(Tony is up and between them.)*
TONY. Sit the fuck down; both of you! I said sit down Torch! I ain't playing. And Mikey, you better check yourself. Go stick your head out the window for a minute; you need some air. *(Mike moves to the window.)* Alright now Mike, I need

take your time, man, ... take your time and break it down.

TORCH. Faggot-ass motherfucker.

TONY. And you keep your fucking mouth shut. I'm trying to get the picture here.

TORCH. Calling me stupid ... you're stupid. Fucking guy could have killed us both.

TONY. Hey why don't you just be quiet!! Come on Mikey ... talk to me man.

MIKE. Okay, okay. We got to the Chelsea hotel about four o'clock. Case the joint, you know? Like we used to do back in the day when we flim-flammed all them Wall Street types. Booked a room on the third floor, went back downstairs and waited at the bar for Manny's people to show. We was supposed to meet at five thirty right? But round about five o'clock, these two cats show up that I ain't never seen before. Young cats man, real young. Couldn't have been no more than 17, 18 years old.

TORCH. Had on them baggy clothes, hats to the back. Fucking straight up stick-up kids.

MIKE. I told Torch to go to our room and wait for the call. Then I caught the elevator with the stick-up kids and rode up to the fourteenth floor. They was babies, man. I couldn't believe it. When we was that age, we never handled the kind of weight these two were dealing. They was riding in an elevator with four kilos of heroin and they looked like they was still on they mama's tittie. We got to the fourteenth floor; they broke left, I broke right. I could feel them clocking me, but I never looked back.... Just kept walking like I was going to my room. I heard them turn the key in the lock and close the door. Ping, ping, my 20/20 told me what room it was, right?

TONY. Fucking guy got eyes in the back of his head.

MIKE. Yeah, but I eased down the hall checking every room for noise, just to make sure. When I got to 1406 I could hear them next door. They turned the TV up full blast, soon as they got in there. I couldn't believe Manny would send such young, dumb, motherfuckers to deal all that weight. But I figured it would make the job easier. So I knocks on the door and they let me in; frisk me, ask who I got with me, that type shit. I ask to see the product and they break out the briefcase and show it to me. Four keys; just like it was supposed to be. I ask them to turn the TV down while I call my man to bring the buy money. We waiting for Torch and I can see they're getting a little nervous. So, I try to make a little light conversation. You know? Try to chill them out by telling them how professional they are. How Manny's always bringing up new talent ... that he's a real stand-up guy and how it's a real pleasure doing business with him and his people. They seemed to calm down a little bit after that. Then Torch knocked on the door. The kid that let him in was a little surprised to see that we was together. But he checked himself when you told him you had Manny's money.

TORCH. Let me tell you something. Money talks and bullshit walks.

MIKE. That's exactly why the shit went wrong man. You wasn't cool. You came in sweaty, with your jaws all tight,

TORCH. The fucking guy was reaching for his piece Mike!!

MIKE. You spooked them man!! Look I ain't saying it's all your fault, but ... I know, I know after you put the briefcase down the kid reached into his jacket.

TORCH. That's right.

MIKE. Yeah but if you had only stayed cool!! If you had just chilled, all you had to do was chill, he never would have fired on us, man.

TORCH. Get the fuck out of here!! You don't know that.

MIKE. I do know. I know because I done it. Me and Tony done it plenty of times. We made over a hundred and fifty grand in less than a year running the same flim-flam on lots of people man.

TORCH. Yeah, but you got busted though.

MIKE. Anyway.

TORCH. Anyway.

MIKE. I could see that the one kid was reaching for his piece but I didn't think he would really pull it out, I swear to God I didn't! I saw Torch go for his and I didn't know what else to do so I grabbed the briefcase and tried to take

it away from the one who was trying to open it. We was standing there fighting for it in the middle of the room and the next thing I know Torch and the other kid started shooting.
TORCH. You should have seen it man, it was like something out of the twilight zone. Bullets were flying, blood was everywhere. I must have shot this kid like 5 fucking times. Everything was moving in slow motion. All you could see was smoke and the whole joint smelled like gun powder. I didn't even know I was shot at first. Felt more like something burned me.
TONY. Okay ... then what happened?
MIKE. The briefcase came open when me and the one kid was fighting for it. That's how we lost one of the four keys.
TORCH. Excuse me, excuse me. I tried to pick up what was left. But the shit was everywhere; it was all mixed up with the shooters blood and whatnot. Tasted like some very high quality shit, though.
MIKE. So we grabbed the rest of the shit and got the fuck out of there. We caught the subway out to Far Rockaway ...
TORCH. I should've capped that other kid, Mikey ... he seen us, he could rat us out.
MIKE. You see, Tony? You see what I'm talking about? You're fucking crazy, Torch, you know that?
TORCH. Well, I ain't sorry for what I did. Cocksucker almost shot my fingers off. It was a do or die situation Mikey. I did and he died. Forget about it. *(Torch is shivering again and his nose is running.)*
MIKE. He's fucking crazy. I can't believe I let myself get into this shit.
TORCH. What's done is done, what are you gonna do? *(Pause.)*
TONY. Hey Torch, you okay man?
TORCH. Yeah, I'm fine. It's just this fucking cold, that's all.
MIKE. Jesus, you had the same fucking cold since I met you. You got to take better care of yourself.
TORCH. Yeah, I know. Remember the old man used to say if you got your health you got everything?
MIKE. No. I wouldn't remember that.
TORCH. Oh yeah, right. I guess you wouldn't. *(Pause.)*

TONY. So now what?
MIKE. I don't know. That's why I called you.
TONY. You robbed somebody like Manny Rivera and you ain't got no getaway plan?
MIKE. We did.... Fuckin Freddy ... he was supposed to meet us out in Far Rockaway. We was supposed to hook up after, catch a plane, get the fuck out of Dodge ... fucking left us hanging.
TORCH. Let me tell you something, we waited an hour and a half at the train station in Far Rockaway for that asshole.
MIKE. Fucking Freddy.
TORCH. You don't worry about it. I'll fucking take care of him.
MIKE. You already took care of somebody.
TONY. Hey, hey, shut up!!! *(Pause.)* Freddy who?
MIKE. Nine-Lives.
TONY. Fucking Freddy Nine-Lives. Aw no wonder he didn't show up. Mikey what made you think you could trust that motherfucker man? We never trusted him before.
MIKE. I know we didn't ... and I know you never liked him, but we used to get all our flim-flam victims from him.
TONY. Yeah, I know. But didn't you ever wonder what it would take for him to set us up. I mean didn't you never stop to think that maybe it was him who dropped dime on us when we got busted?
MIKE. Yeah. But all them lawyers and models and people like that he used to set up for us to vic; come on man. We must have flim-flammed like forty, fifty people in the same year. They had our descriptions and what-not in every precinct downtown. Remember what that cop said when he booked us?
TONY. Yeah, he said we'd been real busy. But yo, if I was you I wouldn't have taken Nine-Lives word for shit. Especially not about Manny Rivera.
TORCH. Why the fuck not? The dope was there like he said it would be. The two guys, the hotel, the time. Everything was like he said it would be. Except for this.
TONY. Did he tell you he used to work for him?
TORCH. Who, Freddy?

TONY. Yeah, Freddy Nine-Lives went to work for Manny after we got out of Rikers. You remember hearing a couple of years back about some Jamaicans trying to kill him?
TORCH. That was the time he took a bullet in the ass. Never forget that one.
TONY. Yeah, well I heard it wasn't no Jamaicans tried to kill Nine-Lives; I heard it was Manny.
MIKE and TORCH. Get the fuck out of here.
TONY. Look, Nine-Lives was working right over here in Tompkins Square, selling jumbos, talking shit and putting all kinds of Manny's business in the street. Now everybody and they mama know that Manny Rivera don't play that shit. He eased up on him one night and put a bullet dead in his ass. I don't blame him, I know he must have wanted to kill him right then and there. But you know Manny is superstitious. I guess he figured, if God and everybody else who's tried to kill Nine-Lives ain't managed to kill Nine-Lives, ain't no reason for him to fuck with it.
TORCH. You say Manny tried to kill Nine-Lives; he says it was Jamaicans. So what; big deal. What's the difference who tried to kill him? Fucking guy is still alive.
TONY. Man they ain't even invented the kind of shit that can kill Freddy Nine-Lives. *(Pause.)*
TORCH. Where'd you hear all this?
TONY. I heard it around.
TORCH. What do you mean you heard it around?
TONY. Around!! You know? Around!!
TORCH. No I don't know, around the corner? Around the block, what?
TONY. Hey, what's your problem?
MIKE. Yeah ... lighten up Torch ...
TORCH. No ... no problem, bro, I just want to know where he heard about Nine-Lives. You said he was out of the life remember? So how's he know? *(Pause.)*
MIKE. Yeah, Tony ... where'd you hear all this?
TONY. Come on, Mike you know how it is. I come to the city sometimes with my old lady. You know Maxine, she likes the restaurants, the shops and whatnot over here. I run into

people from back in the day ... I hear things.
TORCH. Hears things ... fucking hears things. You hear that, Mr. Williams?
MIKE. What?
TORCH. Fucking rat is what.
MIKE. Where?
TORCH. Right here bro ... your friend. *(Mike pulls Torch to the side.)*
MIKE. What are you talking about Torch?
TORCH. What's the matter Mikey your 20/20 ain't working. I told you I'd seen him before.
MIKE. You sure?
TORCH. Yeah, I'm sure.
MIKE. You positive?
TORCH. Absolutely. Absolutely Positive.
MIKE. Where? *(Torch moves toward Tony.)*
TORCH. In Washington Square Park, but you wasn't with the old lady, was you?
TONY. You know who I was with punk. *(Tony pushes Torch away.)*
MIKE. Yo!! Fellas hold the fuck up! Somebody tell me what's wrong?
TORCH. He's wrong Mike, dead wrong. Him and Nine-Lives, I seen them together, dealing in the park. They were both working for Manny. Who's stupid now?
TONY. Mike, I can explain man I ...
TORCH. No, no, no, too late for that. Give me the piece Mikey, where's the piece?
TONY. Mike you got to listen to me ...
MIKE. T, you working for Manny?
TONY. No!! But I was, I was working for him for a while.
TORCH. You see, I told you. He just said so himself he's working for him.
TONY. Worked, I said worked, as in before not now stupid!! *(Torch throws a TV at Tony.)*
TORCH. You're dead, you hear me? Dead!
TONY. I'm right here punk! I'm right here!! *(Mike is between them.)*

MIKE. Yo, Tony, chill. Take it easy Torch.
TORCH. Fuck easy! You take it easy. I told you I didn't like this fucking guy the minute I laid eyes on him. Now he tells us he works for Manny and you want me to take it easy? *(Mike moves Torch away from Tony.)*
MIKE. Okay.... Okay, easy, Billy ... easy. You're right, you're right, we got to find out what's going on. But we got to be cool. Right? We got to be cool. Look at you. You all sweaty and shit. You're gonna make yourself bleed to death. Just sit down and be cool. Tony says he's not working for Manny no more. Right T? *(Tony nods his head yes.)* But like, you was, right? You and Freddy was working for him, right?
TONY. Yeah. Uh-huh. *(Mike picks up the briefcase.)*
MIKE. Okay. I'm kind of confused. I know I ain't seen you in two, three years but I don't remember you telling me nothing like that.
TONY. Mike, you just got to let me explain ...
MIKE. I remember coming over to Jersey a couple of times; Precious got baptized. You telling me you was out of the life, like you had quit dealing. You and Max had opened up a laundromat, some shit, right?
TONY. Yeah man, that's right ...
MIKE. I don't understand, 'cause now you telling me you was working for Manny. You could understand how I might be a little confused, right? I mean especially after you tell me otherwise when I see you, I mean that shit about being out of the life and whatnot? What happened to all of that?
TONY. All that's true, man. Swear to my mother, all that's true except ...
MIKE. Except what?! *(Mike aims the gun at Tony.)*
TORCH. Except he's a fucking liar.
TONY. Hey, I'm sorry Mike man; I mean I was, but I'm not.... Look, I ...
MIKE. Tony, *sabes que yo te amo como mi sangre,* like you was my own blood; but if you lying to me, swear to God I'll kill you.
TONY. I'm sorry Mike. You got to believe me. I just didn't know ...

MIKE. Stop fucking around and tell me the truth. Are you working for Manny or not?
TONY. No! I'm not. Not anymore.
TORCH. The fuck is that supposed to mean? "Not anymore." Fuck this guy Mike! Fuck him! Let's waste him, take his car and get the fuck out of Dodge while we can. *(Tony's cellular phone rings.)* Come on Mike lets do him!
MIKE. Hold up, hold up.
TORCH. What are you waiting for? Waste him!
MIKE. Wait a second.... Fuck! Yo check the pay phone ... check it out Torch, you see two guys there? *(Torch moves to a window.)*
TORCH. You bet your ass Mr. Williams. *(Mike takes the phone from Tony, starts to answer, then hands it back to him.)*
MIKE. Answer it.
TONY. Hello? Yeah. Yeah. No. Um-mm; not yet. Um-mm. He's right here. *(Mike grabs the phone.)*
MIKE. Listen up, you mother ... Max? Maxine?! How you doing, girl? Nah, we ain't found her yet. Nobody's seen her. Damn, is that Precious? What's wrong? Oh.... Trick or treating ... right.... Hey, I'm sorry, Max, I didn't mean to spoil it for her. Yeah ... uh huh ... I know, but what can I do? Debbie's, you know, she's my sister. I love her. I gotta find her. Maxine, please don't be mad at me. I just didn't know who else to call. Tony will be home soon ... okay ... okay, Max. *(Mike hands Tony the phone.)*
TONY. Yeah baby?... Alright I will.... On my way home Maxine ... Max ... Max listen, we got to go now ... I know, baby ... I love you, too. *(Tony hangs up.)*
MIKE. Maxine sounds good, bro, sounds the same.
TONY. Same old Max.
TORCH. So what, his old lady called him, that don't prove shit. It still don't mean he ain't working for Manny.
MIKE. I know, but we still got to be cool.
TORCH. I'm through being cool, I say we waste him now.
MIKE. Billy, you got to calm down, okay!!
TONY. Yeah, you already got one murder beef hanging over your head and I ain't interested in being the second.

TORCH. The night is young, motherfucker.
MIKE. Talk to me T.
TORCH. That's a gun, punk.
TONY. Alright, alright.
TORCH. Put your fuckin hands down.
MIKE. Tell me something.
TONY. I started working for him after we got out of Rikers. Me and Nine-Lives was slinging jumbos over in Washington Square. I didn't like being around him, but business is business. We had been working together for about a year and it seemed like crack was going down for the count. More and more people was coming to the park looking to score dope. I didn't pay it no mind, because I had built up a good clientele. But Nine-Lives, he started talking out the side of his neck about how Manny was moving out of crack and into dope. He could never stop running his mouth about how much money he was going to be making and about how Manny was going to hook him up with a franchise of his own. Now, you know me, Mike. I kept my mouth shut and went on about my business. Manny heard about all of these wolf tickets that Nine-Lives was selling and decided to cash in on them. I looked up one day and heard that Manny had transferred Nine-Lives over to Tompkins Square. Not long after that was when he got shot in the ass. I had already been thinking about getting out of the life anyway. I wanted to get my shit together. You know? Max was pregnant with Precious at the time and I kind of wanted to be around to see my first born. So, I went up to see Manny to tell him how I was feeling about my situation. He was cool; said "Do what you got to do." So I took my little bit of chump change that I had made slinging them rocks, and stepped the fuck off. Moved to Jersey, found me a little store front, got me a couple washing machines, couple dryers and went into business for myself. I swear to you Mike on my little girl man, I ain't had no further conversations with Manny, Freddy Nine-Lives or anybody else in the life except you. The only reason I didn't tell you, was that I didn't want to let you down. That's the truth Mike. Swear to God. No lie.
MIKE. Word is bond?

TONY. Word is bond.
TORCH. What a fucking fairy tale. Don't believe him, Mike. Don't believe him. He's only trying to save his ass.
MIKE. We gonna have to trust him.
TORCH. Why?
MIKE. Because I say so.
TORCH. Fuck that, look give me the piece, you don't want to do him, I will.
MIKE. How many fucking times I got to tell you? No!! We ain't gonna do it your way.
TORCH. Why the fuck not?
TONY. Look, if I was still working for him, you'd be dead already.
TORCH. Yeah, maybe ...
TONY. Ain't no maybes about it. Plus the longer you sit here it's only a matter of time before Manny finds you.
MIKE. Come on, use your head, think for a minute. Maybe he's telling the truth.
TORCH. Yeah, maybe ... but I ...
MIKE. But nothing, come on, you got to trust me on this, okay? I know Tony half my life, if he says he quit Manny I believe him.
TORCH. Yeah ... yeah, okay we let him live for now, but I still don't like you motherfucker!
MIKE. Torch! Torch! please just try to calm down ...
TORCH. Don't fucking tell me to calm down! I'm not a fucking baby.
MIKE. Okay! Okay at least check the street again. See if our two friends are still there. *(Torch goes to the window.)*
TORCH. Excuse me.
MIKE. Hey yo, Tony, I'm sorry, man.
TONY. You put a fucking gun to my head, Mikey!! Me, man.
MIKE. I know, I know ... I'm sorry, I just got scared for a minute man. I'm sorry bro.
TONY. I don't want no fucking apology, Mike, I just want to get you guys out of here. I'm supposed to be out trick or treating with my little girl, instead of fucking around with you guys.

MIKE. Yeah ... okay, okay ... Tony. Yo Torch, you see anybody.

TORCH. Yeah, they're still there.

TONY. Shit! We gotta figure a way out of this.

TORCH. What do you mean, we?

MIKE. He used to work for Manny, maybe he can give us an idea of what he's going to do about us. Maybe he can buy us some time, okay?

TORCH. Okay, but I still say we get out of here. The sooner the better.

TONY. Too dangerous now, he's probably got 15, 20 guys on the street right now, looking for you.

TORCH. Think he put a contract out on us?

TONY. Naw. He's too proud for that, got too much of the street in him. Probably come kill you himself.

TORCH. Fuck him. Thinks he's fucking Tony Montana *(Pause.)*

TONY. Nine-Lives tell you who the buyer was? Whose dope it was supposed to be?

TORCH. Don't matter whose dope it was, it's ours now. We swiped it fair and square.

MIKE. Some new jack from uptown.

TORCH. Some nobody. Fuckin Nine-Lives, I'm gonna get that motherfucker. Almost lost my hand, look at this shit, Mike.

MIKE. I know, Billy.

TORCH. You know nothing!

TONY. Hey, y'all need to quit beefin and start thinking about getting out of here. *(Pause.)* Hey Mike you got to explain something to me. Why you try to beat somebody for some heroin? I mean, I figured you'd always stay away from that shit 'cause of Debbie being a junkie.

MIKE. I told you before, my sister ain't got a fucking thing to do with this. You hear me Tony? Not a fucking thing! Debbie's clean ... she's clean, you understand!!? She ain't getting high no more.

TONY. She's clean? Oh, I didn't know that ... that's beautiful, Hey how's she doing? I mean like where's she at anyway?

MIKE. Arizona. They got some kind of rehab program out there.
TORCH. Oh yeah, what's it like in Arizona?
MIKE. How the fuck should I know?
TORCH. I thought maybe your sister might call you or write to you maybe. Jesus. It's a normal question. People have families they try to stick close; that's all.
MIKE. Oh, so now you want to talk about family; huh?
TORCH. Forget it.
MIKE. Yeah, I thought so. *(Pause.)*
TONY. So if it wasn't your idea, whose was it? Nine-Lives?
TORCH. No, it was mine.
TONY. That figures.
TORCH. The fuck is that supposed to mean?
TONY. How's your cold, my man?
TORCH. Fuck you
TONY. No, fuck with me. How's your cold, junkie?
MIKE. Hey Tony, what you talking about?
TONY. I'm talking about your boy there. Can't you see he's jonesing?
TORCH. He's lying, Mike. This guy is full of shit. He doesn't know what he's talking about!
MIKE. He ain't a junkie, Tony; he's just got a cold man.
TONY. Wake up bro! It's 65 ... 70 degrees outside and this motherfucker got the chills, nose running like a V-8 engine.
TORCH. I ain't got no tracks, motherfucker. See Mike, I ain't got no tracks.
TONY. What about your feet?
TORCH. What about them?
TONY. I peeped them after you had your little accident. Fucking stupid ass junkie.
TORCH. I should have killed you when I had the chance. *(Tony and Torch wrestle. Tony pins Torch down.)* Get off of me!! Get off of me!!
TONY. Check his feet Mike. You don't believe me, check out his feet.
TORCH. Hey come on Mike. Get him off of me.
TONY. Mike, swear to God I ain't lying man. Just check his

feet. *(Mike removes one of Torch's boots.)*
TORCH. It ain't what it looks like.... Swear to God man ... you gotta believe me. I'm just chippin' that's all. I just got a little chippie.
MIKE. Oh shit!! Why everybody in my family got to be hooked on dope?
TORCH. I ain't hooked bro! *(Pause.)*
TONY. What?! You related to this asshole?
MIKE. He's my brother.
TORCH. Half brother. Fucking prick!
TONY. Shut-up punk!
TORCH. Let me up, let me up, let me up ...
TONY. What's the matter junkie? Sick?
MIKE. Leave him alone Tony.
TORCH. I got to get up, I got to get up ...
TONY. Say please, dope fiend.
MIKE. Tony, leave him alone! *(Tony releases him.)*
TORCH. I'm hurting Mike. I'm hurting bad. You got to help me. You got to ...
MIKE. Sssh ... okay, I got you, I got you. We brothers, right? We got to look out for each other right?
TONY. Damn ... I ain't even know you had a brother, let alone one who was ... well, you know. Hey I'm sorry Mike.
MIKE. Yeah, me too. Fucking story of my life. *(Blackout.)*

Scene 3

2 o'clock in the morning.

It is dark and fairly quiet outside.

TONY. Now a lot of you guys might be surprised at what I'm about to say, and you'll want to know who is this guy that talks so sly, and where did he learn to play? Well I'm about to tell of the way that I failed and the dirty trick that fate played on me. These are swinging sounds that I'm running down so you will dig my history. Last new year's night when the whole scene shone bright and all the gamers were stalking their prey, the code was pure crime under them neon lights, and all the tricks were doomed to pay. Crime suddenly begun as soon as daughters met sons, some of them was only five years old. You know, there's been many, many a night that I had to settle for a bite off of some old molded roll. Wayward daughters for dollars and quarters did sell their youthful selves, and in the morning they woke to find their hearts near broke, crying themselves to death. While the junkies prowl with a tiger's growl, in search of that much needed blow. And the winos cringe on a canned heat binge to find their graves in the snow. Where belles of vice sell love for a price, and even the law gets corrupt. Man, you keep on trying, but nevertheless crying, like Jim, what a bitter cup. But the jungle creed says that the strongest feed off of any prey at hand, and I was branded beast at every feast before I ever became a man. I was young and prancy, pot was my fancy, I was known as the adequate male. How I cursed the day that I made my play for that sidewalk Jezebel. She was a brown skin moll, like a China-doll, walking the path of sin. Up and down she trod, with a wink and a nod, and this bitch I had to win. No it wasn't by chance that I caught her glance, 'cause I meant to steal this dame. And as she giggled at me, I jumped with glee, I says it's time for old Slim to game. Under them neon lights her eyes shone bright and from them a teardrop fell. When I asked her why she began to cry and tell this bitter tale. All about some guy that blacks her eye, takes all the bread she gets. When she lands in jail, he won't go her bail and defies her to call it quits. I said; "Baby, dry them tears and have no fear, for the tender kind lover is here. And I'm staking a claim on all parts of your game and I'm vowing to have no peers." Well she looked at me like a slave set free and said I'll be your woman. And when I left with her, her man didn't stir; sheeeit, I knew I had me one. Now she caught on kind of fast as the months rolled past and we gamed to the bitter end. A better hoe I have yet to know, they claim a dog is a man's best friend. Now she ranked with the best from the east to the west and like, when her boosting hand came down? Many, many a chump got left in the dumps as we stole from out of all them towns. Now I laid and I played off the bread this bitch made, from the coast to old Broadway. My habits were small but my money was tall, I really made this business pay. You know how some bitches cry about the wind being high and the cops being on their trail? About the snow and the sleet being asshole deep and all the pimps can go to hell. Sitting in greasy spoons and jukebox saloons killing a lot of time, sucking on beers and crying hard luck tears while the pimps ain't got a dime. Just sitting and bullshitting, sucking them party pricks. Nodding so tough behind messing with stuff that they miss all the righteous tricks! While you could lap their lid for the lowest bid and set that young ass on fire ... the cheapest young girl you could buy. Digging that cunt for a solid month while it's dope that's been doing all the pimping, but not this triple A broad of mine! She was a sex machine that could walk between raindrops come typhoon, blizzard or gale; stand on a hot brick, she'd turn a trick. Man she'd trick with freaks and creeps and toenail freaks, breeds I can't even name. Eskimos, Negroes, Jews, Apache and Sioux; to her it was all the same. Anywhere she would follow that righteous dollar, to hell if she had to go, and be down there waiting just to trick with Satan, she was really a money making hoe. Why for a lick or a lap of that mellow trap, the tricks did fight a duel, course her longest bread was made by head and Jim how that bitch could chew. The sun didn't set when her cunt wasn't wet and how all of her doors did swing. Like many, many a nut got bust in the girls butt, 'cause the rag didn't mean a thing. All my troubles began when I quit snorting and commenced to hitting. Now you know how that go; I shot up more dough than any one bitch could get. I sold my shack, my Cadillac and the rugs from up off of my flo'. I stole from Ma and Pa and shot up all that dough. My woman cried and damn near died when I ran out with her mink, but I stayed in my role. I stole and I sold everything but the kitchen sink. Down I fell, to the depths of hell, I had put myself in a cross. My habits got tall and my money got small, but the deadliest blow of all ... came when this bitch took ill on short notice and could no longer gin. It was a case of piles and inflamed bowels and for a month she couldn't pee. It was like lock-jaw city, and believe me friends, things looked kind of bad for me. Her head was dead, her ass was red, lips on her cunt was cold. I figured, "What the hell, since the bitch ain't well, I'll get me a wife-in-law." Now, there's this redhead bitch with the hoe-house itch over in Pretty Willie's stable. I'll call up Big Mable and do my best, while you convalesce and get back on your feet again. "Like hell!" she cried, "I'll see you dead before I see you go! May the black coach of sorrow pick your ass up tomorrow if you walk beyond that do'. Now I've ruined my health and a bid for wealth so that you could have your bit. You done went dope-head and shot up all that bread, now you talking that stable shit? But you see, I'm wise to the lines that you pimps drop on the frails, and the games you try to play; and if this shit don't cease like, motherfucker, I'm calling the police and have them carry your ass away." Well I kept on fixing my shit 'cause I was getting ready to split and this is what I said; "Bitch, you ain't no lame. You know the game, they call it cop and blow. You done had your run and now you're done. I got to find me another hoe. Wouldn't I look silly, with a broke down filly on a track that's way too fast? Besides, a bitch ain't shit without a good man's wit and your thoroughbred days are past. Now I'll put you in charge of my hoe house at large, give you some girls to rule. But you sound like hell, talking about putting me in jail. You must be a goddamn fool. Bitch step aside, and let me slide, hurry up and get off my back. I've got to find me another young hoe who can run this real fast track." While laying on my back, in another hoe's shack, running down my pedigree, we heard a tremendous thunder that shook the door under and I'm wondering, who in the fuck could that be? Just then a policeman walked in with a great big grin fixed in a deadly expression. Wants to know; "Is your name Rock? Pimping Rock? Hurry up and sign this confession." "That's him!" she cried, swinging her arms in the deepest of glee. "That's the dirty son-of-a-bitch with the con-man pitch that made a stinking hoe out of me." Just then a hell of a blow sent me to the floor and I fell into a black repose. When I awoke, my jaw was broke and blood was all over my clothes. That's the tale that I tell from my prison cell sitting here on my bed. Murder one ... possession of a gun ... yeah, I shot that stinking bitch dead. *(Pause.)*

TORCH. Damn. That's fucking cool.

MIKE. Damn!! Yo, Tony, how you remember all that shit.

TONY. Same as you gonna remember to tell me about you and your boy.

MIKE. Aw, come on Tony, the shit is embarrassing.

TORCH. Fuck you:

MIKE. Fuck you, too. *(Tony rises.)*

TONY. Embarrassing, hunh? You two have a good night.

MIKE. No, man, I'm gonna tell you the whole shit. Hand to my mother, I'm gonna tell you the whole shit. *(Tony sits.)* Okay, okay man, damn. It's like this, I had quit this little bullshit job I had doing phone sales.

TORCH. Excuse me, excuse me. Fucking phone *sex.* 976-A-S-S.

TONY. You had a job? Conversatin with motherfuckers? You bullshitting?

TORCH. No, it's true.

TONY. What was you saying? *"Ay, papi, dami un beso, por favor.* You promised me fourteen inches."

MIKE. Come on. I had just walked out on these tightwad

motherfuckers. Hailed a cab, jumps in and told the cat I was going to Brooklyn, right? The cabbie start talking about, "I am sorry, I cannot take you to Brooklyn. Is quitting time in one-half hour. I must go to Queens." Ignorant, non-English speaking motherfucker! So I said, "You can't take me to Brooklyn, take my ass to the police station then." What the fuck I want to do that for? We drove to the precinct in Hells Kitchen. I went to the desk sergeant, told him I wanted to fill out a complaint about how this cabbie accepted me as a fare and then refused to take me to my destination. You know that motherfucker tried to lie on me. Talking about his off-duty light was on. Desk sergeant asked me my name, I told him Michael Williams. Gave him my alias, I ain't never gave a cop my real name in my life.

TONY. Too much crime ...

MIKE. ... too much time.

TONY. That's right.

MIKE. So like, the desk sergeant went to check on something. Told us to please be seated and he'd be right back. So I'm sitting there and I'm feeling like something's getting ready to jump off, you know. But I can't figure out exactly what. Sergeant came back and called the cabby over; starts whispering to him and shit. So like, on the inside, I'm bugging out, right. But I'm trying to stay cool, you know. Trying to maintain like I'm an upstanding citizen and shit, right. Next thing I know, they shaking hands and shit. The sergeant is apologizing to this hack driving motherfucker for the inconvenience. So I jumps up from my seat like, what the fuck is wrong? The sergeant says; "If you'll follow me this way Mr. Williams, I think we can get this all straightened out." All polite and what not. I should have known right then and there what was happening man. But I was so pissed-off, my 20/20 wasn't working. He took me into one of them interrogation rooms; start giving me the drill: name, address, D.O.B., that type of shit. That's when it hit me, bro. They had ran a N.C.I.C. check on me, and I hadn't seen my probation officer in like two months. I guess after two years of being on the street I started taking my freedom for granted. Sergeant told me they had issued a warrant

for me, so he had to lock me up. But check it out, that ain't even the worst part. When they was taking me down to the holding cell, the sergeant and this other cop was making jokes about me being the second Michael Williams that they locked up in two days.
TONY. You bullshitting?
MIKE. Word!! I get to the holding tank, there's about fifteen other guys there plus this motherfucker; and I'm positive it's anybody but him that they're talking about. That is until the sergeant calls him over and says; "Hey Williams, I want you to meet somebody. Say hello to your twin brother." Shit was embarrassing.
TORCH. It was no day at the beach for me either pal. Sure as shit wasn't funny.
MIKE. Did you see me laughing?
TORCH. No.
TONY. Hold up.... You both got the same alias?
TORCH. Yeah.
MIKE. My mother named me Michael William after my father who I never knew.
TONY. Hold up.... What's your real name, Torch?
TORCH. Michael William Murphy, Jr.
TONY. Oh shit. Your full name is Michael William Leon?
MIKE. Yeah.
TONY. *(Laughs.)* Ain't that a bitch ... goddamn!
TORCH. What's so fucking funny?
MIKE. Yeah Tony, that shit ain't funny, man.
TONY. Yo, I'm sorry fellas. I'm sorry. It's just; damn y'all two are brothers ... that's beautiful. No, no, that's beautiful.
MIKE. Hey, fuck you Tony man! You don't know how that shit make you feel.
TONY. Hey, yo, I'm sorry man, I'm sorry. So, you two never met before? I mean, y'all didn't know about each other or nothing?
TORCH. Yeah, my mother was always bitching and moaning about how the old man knocked up some girl from the projects in East New York.
TONY. What about you, Mike? You know about him?

MIKE. Yeah.
TONY. Damn. Pops was out.
MIKE. I could kill him for what he did to me and my mother.
TORCH. You and your mother? You and your mother? At least you didn't have to live with him. At least you didn't have to lay awake in bed at night for all the fucking screaming and hollering that went on every time he came home soaked to the gills. You didn't have to listen to that. At least you didn't have to hear your mother crying herself to sleep at night because it was safer for her to lock him out, then it was to let him in. You had it easy. At least he didn't break your mother's heart by knocking up some poor bitch from the projects.
MIKE. Hey! Hey, you can talk about your father any way you want to, okay? But when you talk about my mother, you better show her some fucking respect.
TORCH. What, you think your mother was the only one he was fucking around with? You think she was something special to him? You don't think there's maybe two, three hundred Michael William, Juniors walking around the Tri-State area right now? And you call me stupid ...
MIKE. I hate that motherfucker.
TORCH. Let me tell you something about your old man. When I was in high school I was a complete, fucking ignoramus when it came to reading, writing and arithmetic. But I always got good grades in math. Know why? Because the old man was fucking my math teacher. Yeah, Miss Delvecchio. She had the most tremendous set of jugs I had ever seen in my whole life. Like this, I'm telling you. You should've seen them. I spent so much time watching them tits rise and fall; every time she took a deep breath ... forget about it, I could give less than a marvelous fuck about adding and subtracting. All I could think about was multiplying, I never paid attention to what we were supposed to be learning. Anyway, one day she calls my parents.... Have a meeting about my grades. So the old man comes down to the school and off we go to the guidance counselor's office; Mr. Deavor. We're sitting there; me, the old man, Miss Delvecchio and Mr. D. I'm putting on my

best "father forgive me" face; praying to Jesus, Joseph and Mary that I'll get out of this without taking a beating. After about five, ten minutes of conversation between Miss Delvecchio and the old man about my grades, my attitude, my attention span, whatever; she says to me and Mr. D; "Would you gentlemen step outside and allow me to speak to Mr. Murphy in private." We step outside and right away Mr. D starts in on the way back to class. He's busting my chops about hanging with the riff raff after school. Breaking my balls about how I got to pay more attention to what she's teaching me and less attention to her tits. The only thing on my mind is the beating I'm gonna catch come three o'clock. So I'm sitting in class waiting for her to get back. She's gone for like thirty minutes, 'cause the fifth period bell rang just after she came into the room. I remember thinking to myself that there's something different about her. She was the kind of broad that always seemed uptight, you know? The type that always wore her hair pinned up in a bun. But when she came back from talking to the old man, she was all of a sudden wearing it all down around her shoulders. Like out of no where she's all relaxed right? She's got that well fucked look; you know? And you know what else? She never said another word to me the whole rest of the year. Not a fucking word. Except; "Thank you, Mr. Murphy," when I turned in my tests. Which I just knew I was going to fail. But I never did. It didn't take me too long to figure out that he was banging her regular on the side, and that was the reason I had suddenly become a mathematical genius. Broke my mother's heart and 'cause I knew about it, I could never look at her in the eyes again. Now I ain't gonna sit here and tell you that he didn't give you and your poor mother a hard way to go. But me and my mother put up with more of his bullshit on a day to day basis than you can even begin to imagine. So believe me, Mikey, I know how you feel. Believe me. I do. *(Pause.)*

TONY. Damn, that's fucked up.

TORCH. Hey Mike, I'm sick man, how about letting me have a taste.

MIKE. No ... uh-uh No way I'm gonna let you have any of

that shit.
TORCH. Come on Mike. I'm sick. I only need a little bit man. Just a little bit; my gut's killing me.
MIKE. Sorry, bro. I can't let you do that. It's already bad enough as it is.
TONY. What about his hand Mike. I mean he could probably use a little taste.
MIKE. You stay out of this T. It's between me and my brother.
TONY. I thought he was your half brother.
MIKE. Whatever. Me and him stole the shit, and me and him agreed to sell it and make some money together. We didn't say nothing about shooting it. Did we, Torch.
TORCH. No. No. But I'm sick. I'm sick as a dog, man, I swear to God. *(Torch goes back into the bathroom and vomits.)*
MIKE. Too bad. That's just too fucking bad. Damn. I hate this shit … *(Fade to black.)*

Scene 4

5:00 A.M. Dawn.

MIKE. I still don't see why he's gotta have it.
TORCH. 'Cause I'm not gonna fucking make it without it that's why … I'm not.
MIKE. All you gotta do is make it downstairs.
TORCH. Then what? What then huh? We won't even make it to the nearest fucking subway!! What you gonna do, carry me?
MIKE. All you gotta do is hold on to me and we can walk to …
TORCH. NO! I can't … I can't fucking walk, Mikey!! I can hardly sit up straight as it is for chrissakes. If I don't fix soon, I'm gonna die.
MIKE. Don't say that. You ain't gonna die.

TONY. No, he won't, but you gonna wish he was dead if he don't get straight.
MIKE. It still don't make sense him putting that shit in his veins.
TONY. He might as well ... it ain't like he gonna get no better no time soon without it ... look, we been here almost 24 hours!
TORCH. More like 24 years.
TONY. When's the last time you fixed?
TORCH. It's been more than 24 hours!!!... Come on Mikey I'm sick man!!!
MIKE. God, why I gotta have a dope sick junkie for a brother.
TONY. You don't want him to be sick? You gotta let him fix.
TORCH. Yeah Mike, he's telling you the truth ... I just. I just gotta have a hit and ... and I'll be good as new you'll see.
MIKE. I can't fucking stand this shit ... look at you!!
TONY. You ain't got no choice; he's sick, he can't help himself!
TORCH. You gotta listen to him, Mike. I gotta get well ... I'm gonna die if I don't ... swear to God, Mike, I'll die without it ...
MIKE. Fucking stop that shit will you, cut it out, you making me sick to my stomach!!
TONY. Mike ... Mikey man, you gotta get real. I mean it ain't like you got time to play Florence Nightingale while he kicks. *(Pause.)*
MIKE. Okay! Okay! Go ahead.... Go ahead and put that fucking poison in your body. Why the fuck should I care, you only my half brother anyway. I don't even know why I thought that shit meant anything to me.
TORCH. You won't be sorry, bro. I'm serious, you gonna see ...
MIKE. Hey!! Don't you ever call me that again.
TORCH. I'm sorry, bro.
MIKE. You heard what I said!

TORCH. I mean Mike ... Mikey, I'm sorry, alright? I won't call you nothing you don't want me to okay?
MIKE. Why you doin this to me, hunh?
TORCH. I just ... I just want to ...
MIKE. The fuck's the matter with you?
TORCH. I just want to say thanks for letting me take care of my chippie.
MIKE. Why you doin' this to me? First my sister ... now this fucking shit ...
TONY. You got your works, baby?
TORCH. Yeah ... in my jacket. *(Tony opens the briefcase.)*
TONY. Why is one of these keys busted up?
MIKE. What?
TORCH. I had to have a little something, man, while you was checking the roof. Otherwise, I would have shit myself too. I only took enough to keep me from being sick.
MIKE. Shut the fuck up.
TONY. Yo, Mike, chill ... *(To Torch.)* it's okay, we gonna get you straight now, okay?
MIKE. Hey yo, T. I got an idea.
TONY. What's up?
MIKE. Maybe you could call Manny, try to cop us a plea.
TONY. I don't think that's a good idea.
MIKE. Why not, you said he was cool with you when you wanted to get out of the life.
TONY. Yeah, but that was different. I was working for him, I didn't try to rip him off. Besides ... the fuck am I supposed to say? Like, yo Manny, I found your dope and guess what? The two guys who stole it, one of them's my old running partner and the other one's his long lost brother. I don't think so.
TORCH. Aw fuck ... fuck ... my fucking hand don't work! Hey guys, I can't cook the shit up without my hand. One of youse gotta help me.
MIKE. Don't you even fucking look at me. I hope that shit kills you.
TORCH. Don't say that.
TONY. I got it, baby, what you need?

TORCH. I just need you to hook it up for me ... my hand don't work so good no more.
TONY. Okay ... like this?
TORCH. Yeah that's good, that's good, hey thanks Tony man. I mean like I'm sorry about throwing up.... It's just that when I'm sick like this ... I can't ... I can't help it ... I just can't help myself.
TONY. No problem ... no problem baby. *(Tony hands Torch the needle. He moves to the briefcase, closes it, then moves to the window.)*
TORCH. Hey Mike. I'm sorry ... about pissing myself you know. I didn't mean to embarrass you in front of your friend. It's just when I'm sick you know? Hey why you looking at me like that huh? Why you looking at me like.... Come on Mikey stop it.... Don't look at me like that alright? Come on, stop it. Stop fucking looking at me like that!!! I can't stand it when people look at me that way.
MIKE. Why you do that shit anyway?
TORCH. I don't know, 'cause it's all I got.
MIKE. That's bullshit!!
TORCH. *(Fixing.)* No, it's not bullshit! You're bullshit ... you're bullshit man. Oh no I almost forgot you're my brother, my long lost half brother. But what the fuck else have I got? Huh Mikey? You tell me what else have I got. I got no real family. My mother washed her hands of me the second time she found me passed out in the bathroom with a needle stuck in my arm. The old man's been dead longer than I can remember. So what else have I got? I got no job, and I ain't been able to keep one in the past five years. Last job I had I missed so many work days from being sick I just said fuck it and started stealing full time to support my habit, you know? That's part of the reason I started hitting myself in the feet; this way I don't have to go around wearing long sleeves all the time. It does get a little messy sometimes walking around with blood dripping out of your shoe, but it's easier to hide. You want to know why Mikey? You really want to know why I shoot dope? It's because I have to!... It calls?... I come!... I don't? I get sick! You ever been sick? I mean so sick that your

whole body aches and your gut feels like it's on fire? Like your blood's boiling and there's not a fucking thing in the whole wide world you can do about it. Let me tell you Mikey, it's not a good feeling bro. Looking at me like that, fucking 20/20 my ass, yeah you got eyes in the back of your head alright. You got any idea what it feels like to want to quit and know that you can't? I mean like you really, really want to but you just can't. Like, in the past five years alone I've tried to kick three different times; cold turkey the first time. Wound up in the psyche ward at Bellevue with so many cuts and bruises on my hands, my arms, my face ... my own mother didn't even recognize me. Next two times I tried a ten day methadone program over in Brooklyn. They got a waiting list that's stacked up for a whole year ... so between times I just had to do my best to stay high. When I finally did get into the program? I managed to stay clean for seven of the ten days on my first go round, big fucking deal right? The second time, two years later on the eleventh day my girlfriend Patty picked me up and off we went to cop. I had eleven days clean and sixty-dollars when I got out. I bought five bags of dope and a pack of cigarettes. We shot them up just like that. Man I remember the high I got from that shit just like it was yesterday. I mean I felt like a fucking superman, invincible you know? It was one of them able to leap tall buildings in a single bound ... change the course of mighty rivers ... bend steel in your bare hands kind of highs. Then I'd come down and there you'd be looking at me with those eyes. Only it wasn't your face I'd be looking at; it was my own. I'd see my own face in the mirror and start crying and begging for him to let me stop. But he wouldn't, he just kept staring back with this look on his face that's saying; "Who is this crazy strung out junkie staring at me? Can't be who I think it is. I don't look like that do I? This guy looks dangerous ... too dangerous to be out on the street. Too dangerous to be turned loose on society. Too dangerous to be me." But it is you; and you know it. It's you, sure as shit, the way you really are. And what scares you the most is that you know that this is exactly what other people see when they look at you the way you're looking at me.... Hey

Mikey ... I don't feel so good man. *(Torch walks towards Mike and drops dead. Mike moves to him, picks him up, tries to walk him back to life.)*
MIKE. Hey, Torch, stop fucking around, man. Come on, Torch.... Oh, shit. Come on, bro, you gotta walk.
TONY. He ain't gonna make it, man.
MIKE. Don't say that, Tony. Come on, what you sitting there for. Help me. Walk! Come on, Billy; you can do it! Walk.
TONY. Give it up, man. I'm telling you he ain't gonna make it. You wasting your time.
MIKE. You ain't gonna help me? You just gonna stand there and watch him die.
TONY. Man he's dead already. Look at you Mike, you should see yourself. You look like ...
MIKE. Fuck you! *(Pause.)*
TONY. No. Fuck with me. *(Pause.)*
MIKE. What? What you say?
TONY. You heard what I said.... Fuck with me.
MIKE. What the fuck is your problem? You coming off like you don't know me no more!
TONY. That's just it; I do know you, Mike. I know you too well and what hurts me the most is that you ain't changed one fucking bit since I last seen you.
MIKE. How you sound?
TONY. Come on Mikey, you ain't stupid, man! I know you blind when it comes to your people ... but now ain't the time to play stupid.
MIKE. Look, are you gonna help me or not? Come on Tony you supposed to be helping me!!
TONY. Supposed to be, ain't this a bitch!!
MIKE. What?
TONY. Supposed to be my dope. Yeah, the dope you stole is mine! *(Pause.)*
MIKE. You said you wasn't working for Manny?
TONY. I'm not. I got my own franchise over in Jersey. Manny's my supplier.
MIKE. But you said ... you said was out of the life.
TONY. Come on, Mikey. Once in the life, always in the life,

you know the game.
MIKE. Oh shit ... Billy, you was right. I can't believe I trusted you!
TONY. I trusted you, too, Mike! Trusted you with my life. All the scams, the flim-flams, the days we did in Rikers.
MIKE. I need you to help me right now, Tony!
TONY. I want to, but ... besides killing you myself, I don't know what else I can do for you.
MIKE. You gonna kill me? Tony, you gonna kill me, man?
TONY. I don't know ... I mean when I came up here that's what I had set in my mind to do.... But shit, man ... I don't know anymore.
MIKE. You don't know? Come on Tony, you just now said you was gonna kill me. Me.... Godfather to your first-born! Remember me? I can't believe that you'd kill me over some dope. I know you more than half my life. You like family to me. From Erasmus Hall, to the flim-flam, to Rikers Island, the whole nine. Too much crime ... too much time.... Like this! Now you standing here telling me that all of that shit don't count? Like it don't mean nothing? Like all of a sudden I'm some fucking stranger don't mean shit to you no more? I can't believe that.... I mean, I know a lot of shit can happen in two, three years; people change and whatnot; but what the fuck happened to you?
TONY. The world happened, the fucking world happened to me!! I got a criminal record and the world don't want no parts of me, don't give a fuck about me, and don't owe me shit! Not a goddamn thing! So I did what I had to do, now I don't owe nobody a damn thing. Least of all you.
MIKE. Yeah, nobody except Manny. You owe him; motherfucker owns you.
TONY. No, motherfucker, you owe me!
MIKE. I'm sorry about the dope, man, but I didn't know it was yours. Talk to Manny, maybe he ...
TONY. Manny ain't interested in no conversations about nothing. Look, that kid you killed was his nephew.
MIKE. It wasn't my fault. I mean I didn't know.
TONY. Manny don't give a marvelous fuck about whether

you knew or not. He's sitting in a bar three blocks from here and he ain't leaving till he hears from me. Them two cats standing by the pay phone? If I don't take care of business up here with you, they'll take care of it for me and then they'll take care of me. This ain't Erasmus Hall, it ain't no flim-flam, and it ain't Rikers Island. This is the life. What you think he's gonna do to me if I don't come through? What do you think he'll do to Maxine and my little girl?

MIKE. Max? They got Max? They got Precious.... I'm sorry, T.

TONY. No, you full of shit! Talking all this pretty shit about us being friends, coming up together. If you was my friend, you'd go downstairs and handle your business like a man ...

MIKE. I'm sorry, Tony.... I thought ...

TONY. You thought what? Thought you could beat Manny? Thought you could trust Nine-Lives? See, that's your fucking problem. You don't think, Mike. You never did. Had you been thinking, you never would have hooked up with this dead motherfucker here! Fucking junkie had enough heart to face the truth. But you, 20/20 Mike, running around like a blind man.

MIKE. You lied to me.

TONY. No ... you lied to yourself. Told yourself you owed a dope fiend your life 'cause he's your half brother? You don't even know this motherfucker, man!! Mikey, he was gonna sell you out for three keys of skagg. Yeah that's what him and Nine-Lives had planned for you, my brother.

MIKE. Fuckin Freddy Nine-Lives.

TONY. Oh, but don't worry about Nine-Lives. He finally used all them shits up.

MIKE. I ain't ready to die today, Tony.

TONY. And I ain't ready to die for you.

MIKE. Okay ... okay ... okay, look I'll make a deal with you. Bet? *(Tony pulls the gun on Mike.)*

TONY. Fuck a deal. It's do or die time, Mikey.

MIKE. Okay!!! I'll go downstairs!!! Okay? I'll go downstairs!! Look you got to do something for me.

TONY. Mikey, man, I ain't trying to hear you ...

MIKE. I'm gonna go downstairs like you said, okay? I'm gonna go downstairs, but.... I'm gonna try to make it by these two guys.
TONY. Fuck that!
MIKE. *(Mike sinks to his knees.)* No, no, no.... Come on man, listen to me. Just listen to me. Okay ... if I make it, I need you to stall Manny for me for as long as you can. Okay?
TONY. I'm sorry, Mike, I can't do that.
MIKE. I'm begging you. Tony ... please don't kill me!!! Please don't kill me. *(Pause.)* Tony?
TONY. Get up.
MIKE. Huh?
TONY. Get up, Mike. *(Mike rises.)* I don't even know why I'm doing this?
MIKE. 'Cause I'm your boy. Too much crime ... too much crime, yo!
TONY. Yeah.... What the fuck am I gonna tell Manny?
MIKE. You smart. You'll think of something. *(Pause.)*
TONY. Yeah, well if we gonna do this, we got to do it now.
MIKE. Yeah ... do or die time, right?
TONY. Right, right.
MIKE. I'm gonna go out the back. You check the window ...
TONY. Yo, Mike.
MIKE. Yeah?
TONY. You take care of yourself.
MIKE. Yeah, you give Precious a big hug from Uncle Mikey.
(Mike exits. Tony moves to the window; waits a beat and then we hear Mike's footsteps coming downstairs. Tony listens a few beats and moves toward the exit. He calls.)
TONY. Hey Mike.
MIKE. *(Offstage.)* Yo!
TONY. What you gonna do? They're still at the pay phone.
MIKE. *(Offstage.)* I know, I seen them. I'm gonna jump out a back window on the second floor.
TONY. Alright.... Yo, hold up a minute.
MIKE. *(Offstage.)* What? Oh shit!!
TONY. You alright?
MIKE. *(Offstage.)* Yeah, I thought I saw a fuckin rat! What's

up, T?

TONY. You almost forgot your piece.

MIKE. *(Offstage.)* Oh fuck it's dark down here.... Thanks, Tony.

TONY. No problem ... here ... *(Tony levels the gun at the doorway, he fires once.)* Take this. *(Tony fires twice more. He lowers the gun and stands still for a long time. He crosses into the room, picks up his phone, crosses to the window and looks out. He crosses back to the table, lights the candle, picks up the bottle of rum and takes a swallow. He pours the remaining rum onto the floor. He crosses to the briefcase, picks it up, waits a moment, crosses to the doorway and exits.)*

CURTAIN

PROPERTY LIST

Black briefcase (MIKE) with:
- small handgun (MIKE, TORCH, TONY)
- 3 kilos of heroin (TORCH)
- needle

Pillows (MIKE)
Cellular telephone (TONY)
Bottle of rum (TONY)
Six pack of Coke (TONY)
Chinese take-out food (TONY)
Television (TORCH)
Candle (TONY)
Lighter or match (TONY)

SOUND EFFECTS

Faint street sounds (traffic, sirens, shouts, etc.)
Loud screeching
Cellular phone ring

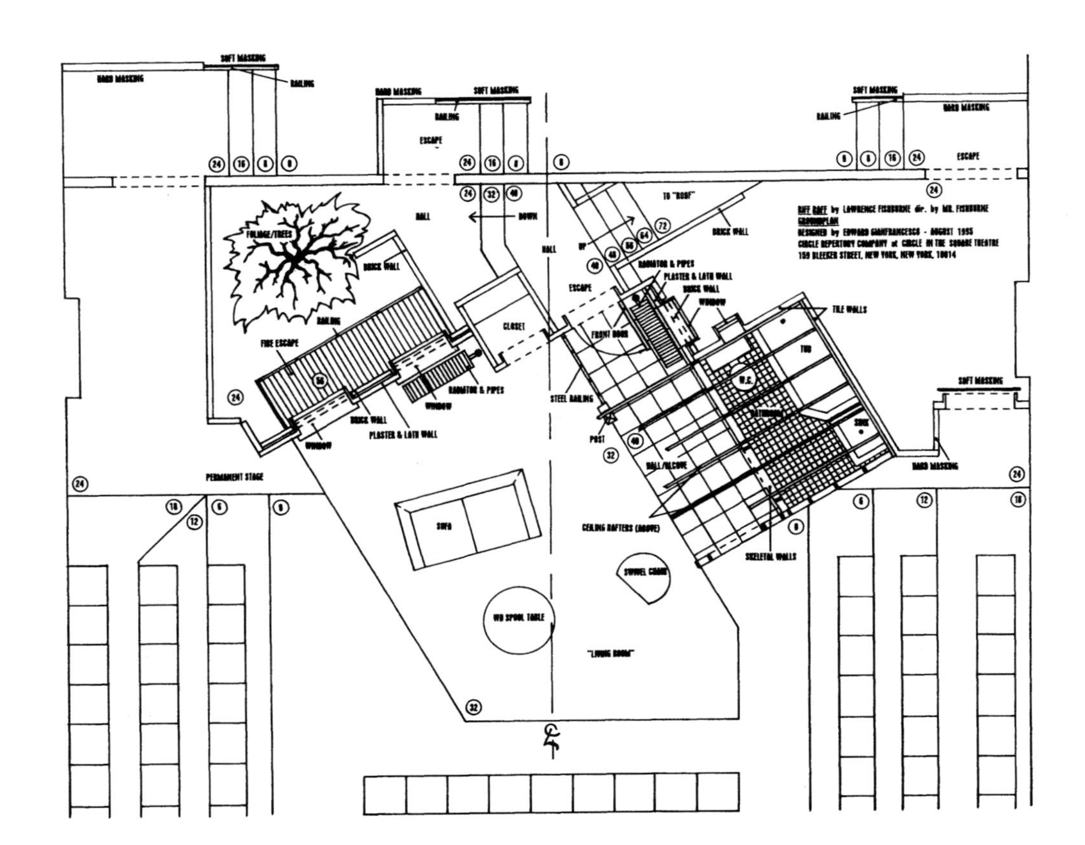
HARD MASKING
SOFT MASKING
RAILING
ESCAPE
HALL
DOWN
UP
TO "ROOF"
BRICK WALL
FOLIAGE/TREES
RAILING
FIRE ESCAPE
WINDOW
PLASTER & LATH WALL
RADIATOR & PIPES
CLOSET
STEEL RAILING
FRONT DOOR
POST
HALL/ALCOVE
TILE WALLS
TUB
W.C.
SINK
SKELETAL WALLS
CEILING RAFTERS (ABOVE)
SOFA
SWIVEL CHAIR
WD SPOOL TABLE
"LIVING ROOM"
PERMANENT STAGE
RIFF RAFF by LAWRENCE FISHBURNE dir. by MR. FISHBURNE
GROUNDPLAN
DESIGNED by EDWARD GIANFRANCESCO - AUGUST 1995
CIRCLE REPERTORY COMPANY at CIRCLE IN THE SQUARE THEATRE
159 BLEEKER STREET, NEW YORK, NEW YORK, 10014

NEW PLAYS

★ **AUGUST: OSAGE COUNTY by Tracy Letts.** WINNER OF THE 2008 PULITZER PRIZE AND TONY AWARD. When the large Weston family reunites after Dad disappears, their Oklahoma homestead explodes in a maelstrom of repressed truths and unsettling secrets. "Fiercely funny and bitingly sad." *–NY Times.* "Ferociously entertaining." *–Variety.* "A hugely ambitious, highly combustible saga." *–NY Daily News.* [6M, 7W] ISBN: 978-0-8222-2300-9

★ **RUINED by Lynn Nottage.** WINNER OF THE 2009 PULITZER PRIZE. Set in a small mining town in Democratic Republic of Congo, RUINED is a haunting, probing work about the resilience of the human spirit during times of war. "A full-immersion drama of shocking complexity and moral ambiguity." *–Variety.* "Sincere, passionate, courageous." *–Chicago Tribune.* [8M, 4W] ISBN: 978-0-8222-2390-0

★ **GOD OF CARNAGE by Yasmina Reza, translated by Christopher Hampton.** WINNER OF THE 2009 TONY AWARD. A playground altercation between boys brings together their Brooklyn parents, leaving the couples in tatters as the rum flows and tensions explode. "Satisfyingly primitive entertainment." *–NY Times.* "Elegant, acerbic, entertainingly fueled on pure bile." *–Variety.* [2M, 2W] ISBN: 978-0-8222-2399-3

★ **THE SEAFARER by Conor McPherson.** Sharky has returned to Dublin to look after his irascible, aging brother. Old drinking buddies Ivan and Nicky are holed up at the house too, hoping to play some cards. But with the arrival of a stranger from the distant past, the stakes are raised ever higher. "Dark and enthralling Christmas fable." *–NY Times.* "A timeless classic." *–Hollywood Reporter.* [5M] ISBN: 978-0-8222-2284-2

★ **THE NEW CENTURY by Paul Rudnick.** When the playwright is Paul Rudnick, expectations are geared for a play both hilarious and smart, and this provocative and outrageous comedy is no exception. "The one-liners fly like rockets." *–NY Times.* "The funniest playwright around." *–Journal News.* [2M, 3W] ISBN: 978-0-8222-2315-3

★ **SHIPWRECKED! AN ENTERTAINMENT—THE AMAZING ADVENTURES OF LOUIS DE ROUGEMONT (AS TOLD BY HIMSELF) by Donald Margulies.** The amazing story of bravery, survival and celebrity that left nineteenth-century England spellbound. Dare to be whisked away. "A deft, literate narrative." *–LA Times.* "Springs to life like a theatrical pop-up book." *–NY Times.* [2M, 1W] ISBN: 978-0-8222-2341-2